RESPONSES

WHAT DO YOU THINK?

Barbara Wintersgill with Janet Dyson

Longman

HOW TO ASSESS YOUR OWN WORK

You can do the following exercise as a group, or as individuals, or both. The purpose of it is to help you think about what you are learning as you go along. You can do this after working through a section of the book, or just after one activity.

1 Choose THREE items from list **A** and FOUR from list **B** which best describe what you have been doing.

2 Write down the items you have chosen and explain briefly why you chose each one, giving an example from your work as an illustration of that item, if possible. (For example: 'I chose **A 1** because we spent a lot of time talking about what we would do if we were told to fight in a war. Trevor told us about his grandad who had been in prison because he was a pacifist in the last war, and what he told me made me think a lot.')

3 If you did **1** and **2** as a group activity . . . was there any item which the group agreed on which you would not have chosen for yourself? If so, explain why, and say what item you would have chosen instead. Why do you think you disagreed with the group discussion?

4 Write about, or talk about, any one part of the work you did not particularly enjoy doing. Say why.

5 Write or talk about any part of the work you did enjoy.

6 Of the work you have done in this section, which piece do you think is your best? Why?

A – general

1 We listened to and learnt from each other.
2 We expressed our opinions and supported those opinions with reasonable arguments.
3 We worked well together as a group.
4 We presented our ideas and information clearly in writing.
5 We presented ideas and information to others but NOT in writing.
6 We had to use our imagination.
7 We did some creative work which we were satisfied with.
8 We solved problems.
9 We had to make decisions.
10 We had to explain the meaning of texts (writing).
11 We had to explain the meaning of pictures.
12 We researched new information.
13 We had to apply facts we already knew to a new situation.

B – specialist

1 We had to explain and give reasons for our own opinions and beliefs.
2 We thought about what we would do in a certain situation.
3 We asked questions about other people's beliefs.
4 We thought about other people.
5 We put ourselves into the place of another person in order to understand their point of view.
6 We felt that we could respect each other's views, and the views of other people.
7 We understood how a person's behaviour was affected by what they believed.
8 We made judgements on a moral issue.
9 Some/one of us changed their minds about something.
10 We understood why there can be different solutions to a problem.
11 We suggested how people, including ourselves, might behave in certain circumstances depending on their beliefs.
12 We felt that in some situations it was not possible to make a judgement or reach a decision.
13 We felt that although we reached a decision on a matter, as we get older and found out more, that opinion might change.
14 We decided what the results might be of behaving in a certain way.
15 We tried to understand ways in which humans can affect the world in which they live.
16 We had to think about where our beliefs come from.
17 We had to compare different beliefs or ideas.

CONTENTS

1 CREDO

YOU WILL BE THINKING ABOUT WHAT BELIEFS ARE IMPORTANT TO YOU AND TO OTHER PEOPLE, AND HOW THESE BELIEFS AFFECT THE WAY WE BEHAVE.

BELIEF

Most people believe in *something*. Some people hold such strong beliefs that it affects the way they act and the way they treat other people. In fact, their beliefs affect their whole attitude to the world.

CREDO is a Latin word. It means 'I believe'. From credo we get the word creed. A creed is really a statement about what someone believes. From credo we also get the word 'incredible' which means unbelievable.

Who is this man?
For what beliefs is he well known?
How do his beliefs affect what he does?

If we believe in absurdities we shall commit atrocities.

(Albert Einstein)

What do you think this statement means?

SIX STATEMENTS OF BELIEFS

Read these statements carefully:

- **I believe in God, the Father Almighty, maker of Heaven and Earth.**
- **I believe it's a free country and I can do what I like.**
- **I believe that all people are created equal.**
- **I believe it is wrong to use animals for testing cosmetics and household products.**
- **I believe in looking after NUMBER ONE!**

GROUP WORK

1 Choose any THREE of the statements in the shaded box. In each case, explain what sort of behaviour you would expect from someone who held that belief.

2 Let each individual in the group write down a belief which he or she holds strongly.

3 Take it in turns to read your 'I believe' statement to the rest of the group. Each person must explain why they agree or disagree with each other's statements.

4 Make a neat copy of all your group's 'I believe' statements.

5 As a group, work out what your different beliefs mean to the people who hold them. Discuss together how you think your beliefs affect your lives.
   a) If you held these beliefs, what difference might it make to others around you?
   b) If you held these beliefs, how might they help you live your own life?
   c) How might holding these beliefs make you behave well or badly towards the environment?
   d) If *everyone* held these beliefs, what difference might it make to the future?

WRITTEN WORK

Looking at the beliefs your group has chosen, give your group a name. Write a story about a weekend in the life of your group.

I DO NOT BELIEVE . . .

- I do not believe in the right of the strongest, nor the force of arms, nor the power of the oppressors. I want to believe in human rights, in the solidarity of all people, in the power of non-violence.

- I do not believe in racism, wealth, privilege, or the established order. I want to believe that all men and women are equally human, that order based on violence and injustice is not order.

- I do not believe that I can fight oppression far away if I tolerate injustice here.

- I want to believe that there is but one right everywhere, that I am not free if one person remains enslaved.

- I do not believe that war and hunger are inevitable and peace unattainable.

- I want to believe in the beauty of simplicity, in love with open hands, in peace on earth.

- I do not believe that all suffering is in vain, nor that our dreams will remain dreams.

- But I dare to believe, always and in spite of everything, in a new humanity; in (God's own dream of) a new heaven and a new earth where justice will flourish.

(a modern Christian Creed written by an unknown author in Indonesia)

GROUP WORK

Take each phrase from the creed above and illustrate it carefully. You can do this by making a collage for each phrase from headlines or pictures from magazines and newspapers, or by drawing your own design. Make sure that you write the words of the phrase under the illustration.

DISCUSSION

WHERE DO YOU THINK YOU GET YOUR BELIEFS FROM? Did they suddenly come to you? Could other people or groups have influenced you? See how many things or people you can think of who influence the ideas you have.

IDEAS TO USE WITH CHILDREN   FREE

'I have a dream'

'I have a dream today – that freedom will reign...' Martin Luther King

Christian Aid Week May 16-21 1988

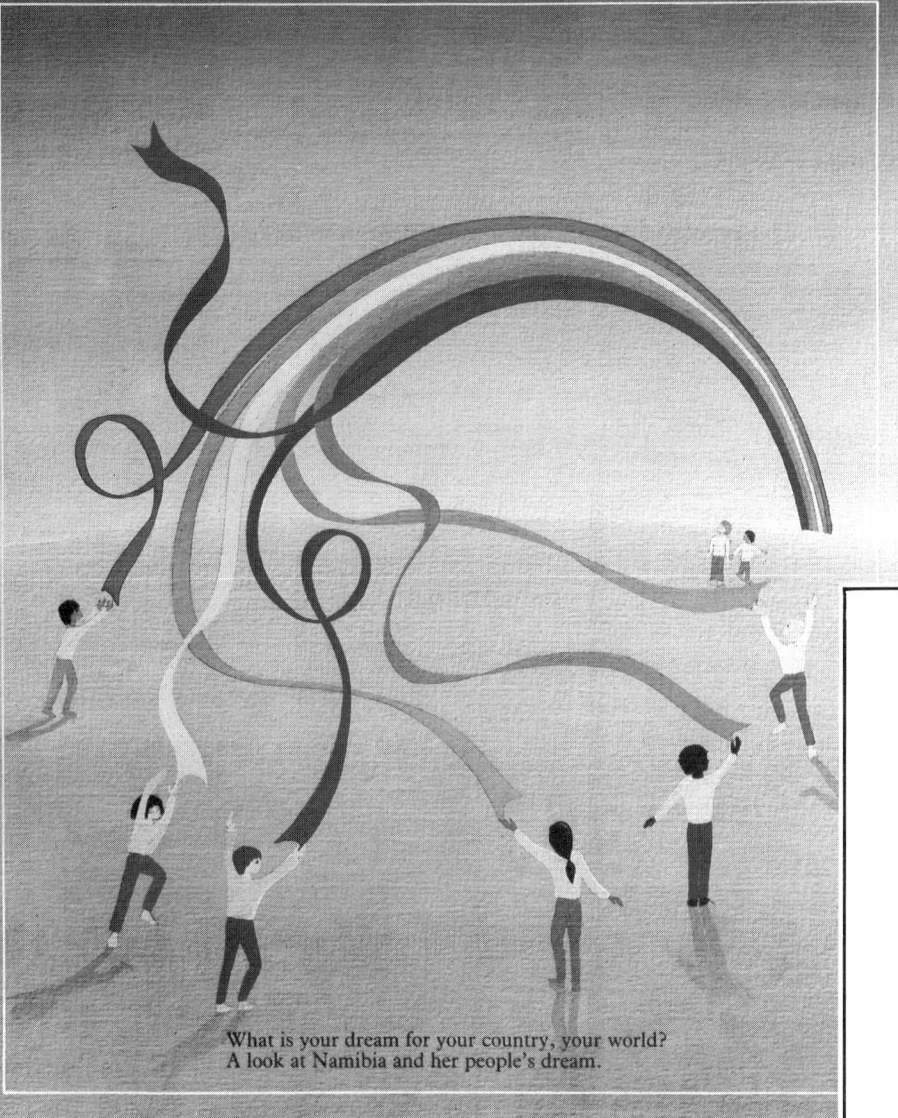

What is your dream for your country, your world?
A look at Namibia and her people's dream.

'I want to believe in the beauty of simplicity, in love with open hands, in peace of earth.'

'I have a dream

'I want to believe that all men and women are equally human, that order based on violence and injustice is not order.'

2 QUAKERS AND PEACE

YOU WILL BE THINKING ABOUT IDEAS SUCH AS PEACE AND SUFFERING.

THINKING ABOUT PEACE

Members of the Society of Friends (sometimes known as the Quakers) have always believed that preparing for war, and the use of violence as a means of solving problems between individuals and nations, are not compatible with the teaching of Jesus. This passage is taken from a document presented by the Quakers to King Charles II in 1660.

RESEARCH

1 What is 'testimony'? Write down three sentences, using the word testimony in a different way in each sentence.

2 What 'outward weapons' would have been used to fight wars in the reign of Charles II?

3 Make a list of all the wars which have been fought during the 20th century. Find out how many people have died as a result of these wars.

4 What are the differences between wars being fought in the 17th century and wars being fought now?

5 Look up the following passages in the Bible. They are frequently referred to as being the authority for Christian belief on the use of violence.
   Matthew 5:38-48
   Matthew 26:52

6 How close to what is in the Bible is the Quaker belief and practice regarding violence?

7 Not all Christians agree with the way the Quakers have interpreted the Bible on the subject of war. Find out what arguments other Christians use to support the use of violence under certain conditions.

Peace Testimony of the Society of Friends

WE UTTERLY DENY ALL OUTWARD WARS and strife, and fightings with outward weapons, for any end, or under any pretence whatever; this is our testimony to the whole world. The Spirit of Christ by which we are guided is not changeable, so as once to command us from a thing as evil, and again to move unto it; and we certainly know, and testify to the world, that the Spirit of Christ, which leads us into all truth, will never move us to fight and war against any man with outward weapons, neither for the kingdom of Christ, nor for the kingdoms of the world.

(From *A Declaration from the Harmless and Innocent People of God, called Quakers,* presented to Charles II, 1660)

MORE ABOUT THE QUAKERS

Quakers believe that something of God is in everyone and that it is wrong to take up arms against anyone – even in wartime. Many Quakers have been imprisoned and persecuted because of their refusal to fight when their country was at war.

In countries where there is conflict, Quakers often act as MEDIATORS (go-betweens or link persons), trying to bring the different sides together.

You will often see Quakers on rallies and peace marches with banners saying 'QUAKERS ARE OPPOSED TO ALL WAR'.

A PRAYER FOR PEACE

This prayer is said at noon every day, all over the world, by people of many religions and by those who have no religious belief. This means that there is never a time when the prayer is not being said.

- What is it about the prayer that makes it possible for it to be said by people of any religion or of no religion?

DISPLAY WORK

Write your own 'Prayer for Peace' which could be said by people of any religion or of no religion. Display your work and read other people's prayers.

PRACTICAL WORK

1 In groups, prepare a school assembly on the theme of PEACE.

2 Write a poem to express your own vision of peace.

3 SAYING 'NO' TO WAR

YOU WILL BE THINKING ABOUT PRINCIPLES SUCH AS PACIFISM AND PEACEFUL PROTEST – AND CONSIDERING WHY THERE IS SO MUCH CONTROVERSY ABOUT THESE ISSUES.

STANLEY JONES – CONSCIENTIOUS OBJECTOR

Pacifism is based on the idea that every individual has the right to decide for her/himself whether to cooperate in a war; pacifists are people who have decided that war is wrong.

Stanley Jones is a Christian who feels that war is not an acceptable way of solving problems; when the Second World War broke out in 1939 he refused not only to fight but to do anything which would in any way support the war. Here he explains why:

I was a year old when the First World War started, a war so terrible that it became known as the 'war to end all wars'. I think that I grew to be a fairly normal boy, fond of games and exercise, but I hated bullying whether I was suffering or not. When I was of an age with the bullies I did my best to make them feel uncomfortable.

One or two young men I knew joined the armed forces but the idea of war was far from anyone's mind – they usually joined because they couldn't get work. 'JOIN THE ARMY AND SEE THE WORLD; MEET INTERESTING PEOPLE,' said the posters. Someone with different ideas of the army's purpose added the words 'AND KILL THEM!' Words can be skilfully used to midlead us.

A film 'All Quiet on the Western Front' vividly reminded us of the horror, misery and sheer waste of war. The actor Lewis Ayres who played a leading part, was so powerfully affected that he refused to fight in the 1939 – 45 War when he was called up. For centuries, people had taken wars for granted but now everybody was affected and, apart from the death and destruction, wars were leaving more problems than they cured. The soldier was told that he could 'show no greater love than laying down his life for a friend'. When Jesus said this I don't think he had soldiers in mind! A better way is to lay down a *lifetime* in service to others. A soldier's job is to kill.

These were the thoughts which influenced me in the years before the Second World War. I was utterly against war as a means of settling problems. I was not prepared to drop bombs on people I didn't know or to do bayonet drill on dummies. Would it be right to do other war work and let other people do the killing instead of me?

When my call-up came I didn't register because I objected to the whole business of arranging destruction and death. Sometimes I have been called a 'pacifist' but I can imagine some situations where I think I would use force or even kill if events forced me, but this would in no way be like organised killing in war. Most people were horrified at the idea of breaking the law as I did and I felt like an outcast. Are there not higher laws than human laws? We live in a glorious world and our duty, surely, is to love and reverence it and the life in it now – or it will be too late.

I lost my job and the magistrates fined me £5 (equal to about £150 today). I refused to pay and was sent to prison where my days were spent in the workshop. Here prisoners and officers were able to talk almost freely.

They thought it something of a joke that the best that could be done with me was to lock me up! When I came out I was ordered to attend a conscientious objectors' tribunal which I refused to do. I had by this time obtained work in agriculture and when the tribunal met in my absence they registered me for work on the land. I wrote to say that this was not acceptable and I would leave such work if I felt it right. They did not dispute this; they were probably relieved to have me placed somewhere and doing something useful, which I believe I did, for over four years.

You may ask who I thought **I** was to feel that I knew better than those who were governing the country! The answer is that I didn't. I felt pretty small and alone but there were some things I just could not do.

(Stanley Jones)

QUESTIONS FOR DISCUSSION

1 What is a bully? Why do you think Stanley Jones links the idea of bullying with his thoughts on war?

2 Look up the word 'pacifist' in a dictionary. Substitute another word for it. (Clue: Matthew 5:87)

3 On what grounds does Stanley Jones object to war as a method of settling disputes?

4 Why do you think the prisoners and officers were amused by the fact that Stanley Jones had been put in prison?

5 'I can imagine situations where I think I would use force or even kill if events forced me . . . '. What sort of events might he be thinking about?

6 *'People living in this country today are reaping the benefits of victory in war in 1945. People like Jones have given nothing to this country, and shouldn't have the nerve to share in the good times now.'* Give reasons for agreeing or disagreeing with this statement.

7 *'It takes more guts to be a conscientious objector than to fight.'* What do you think?

8 Would you be prepared to join the army if conscription were re-introduced? Give reasons for your answer.

9 If there was a war, would you volunteer to fight? Give reasons for your answer.

ASH WEDNESDAY 1987 – GROUP DISCUSSION

1 '. . . charcoal and ashes blessed by priests'. What are these ashes usually used for on Ash Wednesday?

2 What does Ash Wednesday mean to most Christians? Why is it important that this demonstration was taking place on Ash Wednesday?

3 The protest was only supported in writing by three bishops. Write a letter to the Press as it might have been written by one of the non-attending bishops giving reasons for not supporting the demonstration.

4 'We must obey God rather than men.' What were 'men' doing which in the opinion of the protesters was against the will of God?

5 The protesters wrote 'See Acts 5:29' on the wall. What does this passage say? Why do you think it was chosen?

Christians charged after MoD protest

by Martin Wainwright

Forty-five Christian opponents of nuclear weapons were arrested yesterday after scrawling texts and crosses on the Ministry of Defence headquarters with a mixture of charcoal and ashes blessed by priests.

Forty-one were charged with criminal damage and will appear before Bow Street magistrates tomorrow. The protest – on Ash Wednesday, a traditionally Christian day of repentance for the sins of the world – was supported in writing by one Catholic and two Church of England bishops.

The bishops' letters were handed out by some 150 Christians, accompanying those arrested, who included four priests, a hospital consultant, an ex-RAF fighter pilot and at least three grandmothers.

They managed to write 'Repent' and 'Father Forgive Them' on the building and 'See Acts 5: 29' (where St Peter says: 'We must obey God rather than men.')

In his supporting letter, the Bishop of Dudley, the Rt Rev Tony Dumper, wrote: 'Any technical infringement of the law is irrelevant to the real issue, which is how we can better care for God's world.'

The protest, one of the biggest Christian acts of disobedience in recent times, was organised by Catholic Peace Action, Christian CND, the Fellowship of Reconciliation and Pax Christi.

(from *The Guardian*, March 1987)

A woman has written 'REPENT' on a pillar. What does REPENT mean? Who does she think should repent; and why should they need to repent?

A BUDDHIST VIEW

This, O Bhikkus, is the Noble Truth of *Suffering*: birth is suffering; decay is suffering; illness is suffering; death is suffering. Presence of objects we hate, is suffering; separation from objects we love, is suffering; not to obtain what we desire, is suffering. Briefly, the fivefold clinging to existence is suffering.

'WORLD PEACE'

So for us to begin to look at the direct situation is not a question of ceremonies or of religion or Buddhism or any of that nonsense. It demands that we look in some very deep way at the *sorrow and suffering* that exists now in our time, in our world. And to look at our personal and individual and collective relationship to it. To bear witness to it, to acknowledge it, instead of running away. The suffering is so great that mostly we don't want to look. We close our minds. We close our eyes and hearts.

There are two sources of strength in this world. One source of strength is people who aren't afraid to kill. They run a lot of the world, if you look at it from a political point of view. People who aren't afraid to kill run nations, run wars, run much of the world. It gives one a lot of strength not to be afraid to kill. The other source of strength in the world – of real strength – is people who aren't afraid to die. People who have looked into the very source of their nature, have looked in such a deep way that they understand and acknowledge and accept death – and in a way, have died.

(Jack Kornfield)

DISCUSSION

1 The following statements are made by the author, Jack Kornfield. Discuss them carefully, and say whether or not you agree with them.

- The suffering in the world is so great that 'we don't want to look'.
- '. . . people who aren't afraid to kill run nations, run wars, run much of our world.'
- The real source of strength in the world is 'people who aren't afraid to die'.

2 What do you think the writer means when he says that we have a 'collective relationship' to sorrow and suffering?

3 If a person is not afraid to kill, what sort of power might this give them?

4 PEACE PARK

Cartoon showing the aftermath of the American nuclear bombing of Hiroshima – by Kazuhiro Ishizu age 68

Read the article and then answer these questions.

1 Find out (if you don't already know) about the bombings at Nagasaki and Hiroshima.

2 'There is no justice without peace and no peace unless there is justice.' What does this mean? Give an example of both statements.

3 What is seen as the difference between a peace park and a war memorial? Is there a conflict of interest between the two?

4 The article refers to a controversy (argument).
   a) Which two groups are arguing?
   b) Who wants the peace garden, and who does not want it?

Controversial peace park opens

The peace garden at Memorial Park in Bridge of Allan, which has been the subject of intense controversy, was opened at a ceremony on Monday, writes Alison Jenkins.

The dedication ceremony took place in the week of the 40th anniversary of the bombing of Nagasaki and Hiroshima and six survivors of the attack were present.

Their message was simple – 'No more Hiroshimas'.

Around 50 guests, including local church representatives, councillors from various regional and district councils, members of peace groups and a representative of the British Nuclear Tests Veterans Association, were welcomed by Stirling District Council Convener Ian Wyles.

He spoke of the nuclear threat and said the time had come to say 'enough is enough'.

'Things must change and I hope that people all over Britain will bear that in mind this week.

'If people are really concerned about peace and justice they should realise that the two go together. There is no justice without peace and no peace unless there is justice. That is very appropriate in today's ceremony.'

The dedication ceremony was performed by Canon Kenyon Wright, and he referred to the controversy surrounding the siting of the peace garden in the Memorial Park.

'It has been the subject of long and acrimonious discussion and in one way that is quite sad. But the debate has been a good thing because not only has it meant that everyone in the district knows about this place but it has given the opportunity to spell out clearly and unambiguously what this place is all about and why it is important.'

He said that one of the questions raised was the connection of the peace garden with the war memorial.

'We honour the sons and daughters of Bridge of Allan whose names are on that memorial. The peace garden reminds us what these people really died for and far from dishonouring them, it gives new meaning to their sacrifice. We will never forget.'

Canon Wright also spoke of the 'obscene escalation' of nuclear weapons and said he believed they should never be accepted.

One of the six survivors, who were in Stirling as part of a busy tour of the UK, also gave a short speech. Through an interpreter he said he was very impressed with the beautiful park which had been dedicated to peace.

'We are very pleased to be able to attend this ceremony which is a very important occasion for the community. Mankind cannot co-exist with nuclear weapons. We need to work hand in hand for peace.'

He did manage three words in English: 'No more Hiroshimas.'

Another of the survivors was asked to unveil the stone engraved with the symbol of a dove and the words, 'This garden is dedicated to peace'. The stone is the central feature of the peace garden which occupies a corner of the Memorial Park. There are four wooden benches engraved with the word 'peace' which face the trees, shrubs and plants in the garden.

Bridge of Allan Community Council, which was opposed to the siting of the peace garden in the Memorial Park, has not changed its mind. It has accused Stirling District Council of choosing to ignore the voice of the community on the issue which it claims to have expressed 'conscientiously and truthfully'.

(from the *Stirling Observer*, July 1985)

LETTERS TO THE EDITOR

1 Sir – As the proposed peace garden pushes ahead, I can see no sign that local opposition to it has died down.

The widespread view seems to be that Memorial Park belongs to the people of Bridge of Allan, the district council are its trustees, and it should remain as it is, impeccably maintained as a war memorial park. That's what people think and want – in spite of fluent arguments by Convener Wyles and others.

The connection with Hiroshima and Nagasaki has proved emotive and is currently being played down by the district council. I can only point out that my invitation to attend the ceremony on August 5 is headed 'Commemoration of the 40th Anniversary of the Bombing of Hiroshima and Nagasaki'. Commemorate means 'perpetuate the memory of'.

The CND assurance that they do not plan any kind of demonstration and will at all times respect the purpose and nature of the garden as a place of quiet is helpful. But I can only condemn the ease with which CND, a political pressure group, has been able to secure Memorial Park as a peace park against the clear will of the community.

I hope that people who feel angry about the proposal will stay away.

2 Sir – It comes as no surprise that letters not in favour of Bridge of Allan's opposition to the 'peace park' concentrate heavily on the anti-Japanese aspect of the matter.

The community council's objection, and that of most of those who attended the meeting in the Leisure Centre, was to the action of Stirling District Council in making a decision like this without consulting the people of Bridge of Allan.

This behaviour was made even more disgusting by their undemocratic insistence on consulting CND. This body represents neither Bridge of Allan nor Stirling District.

On the Japanese issue, the few people who raised opposition on these grounds were those who had experience of the Japanese in the war. Any 'forgiving and forgetting' can only be done by them. The rest of us may advocate such a course, but we have nothing to forgive.

(from the *Stirling Observer*, August 1985)

3 Sir – The controversy over the proposed peace garden has only served to create a misconception that we have enmity towards Japan, which I'm sure is far from the truth. To further erase this my daughter and son-in-law had Japanese neighbours and harmoniously exchanged interest in each other's language, traditions and art.

Having exploded (non-nuclear I hasten to add) these myths, surely it's down to the fundamental fact we revere our Memorial Park and want it to remain a memorial to men who died so that we could live in peace.

Councillor Michael Connarty shared in the peace and tranquility of the park so why does he find it necessary to dedicate or (dictate) a peace, that, in his own words, is already there!

4 Sir – Thankfully, I was not taken prisoner by the Japanese – I did not even serve in the theatre of war where that might have happened.

I agree wholeheartedly with your correspondent, Mr C A Rankine who did suffer at Japanese hands, and who lived to tell the tale. The destruction of these two Japanese cities and the awful casualties arising from that destruction were very terrible and I would be the last to minimise them, so were the air raids on my home towns of Merseyside, Coventry, Clydebank and London, and for that matter on lovely Dresden.

But the hideous treatment by Imperial Japan on thousands of Allied prisoners of war should never be forgotten. Future generations may eventually forgive, just as Israel has forgiven Germany to an extent, but my generation and Mr Rankine's find that forgiveness well-nigh impossible.

It cannot by stressed too often that had not those two atomic bombs been dropped and so put Japan out of the war in less than a week, few if any of the POWs in Japanese hands would have been allowed to live. This, as Mr Rankine says in his letter, was declared Japanese policy. For this reason, the anniversary of the dropping of these terrible nuclear bombs might justifiably be an occasion for thanksgiving.

I see that religious services of several kinds are to mark the occasion. I am a regular churchgoer, but somehow I don't think I could compromise with my conscience and my faith to the extent of attending.

· PEACE · PARK ·

Many people in Bridge of Allan did not want the peace park. Here are a number of possible objections to the garden. Taking each argument in turn, decide whether this was an argument raised in any of the letters, and if so, which one(s)?

1 The opening ceremony made it look as though the Japanese have been forgiven for their treatment of Allied POWs (prisoners of war).

2 America was justified in dropping atomic bombs on Japan. The garden suggests that they were wrong to do so.

3 The decision to open the park was taken without consulting the people of Bridge of Allan.

4 CND (Campaign for Nuclear Disarmament) should not have been consulted. It was nothing to do with them.

5 The Memorial Park is already a memorial to peace. The council didn't need to open a special peace garden.

6 The peace garden is an insult to the war dead. It suggests that they did not die for peace.

7 The peace garden is a piece of political manoeuvring on the part of the district council.

MR RANKINE'S LETTER

Letter **4** refers to another letter (not printed here) written by a Mr C A Rankine. From the information given:
a) Write Mr Rankine's letter as you think it would have been.
b) Write an answer to the letter by an opponent of Mr Rankine's views.

THE PURPOSE OF THE GARDEN

Which of the following do you think were reasons for making the garden?

- To remember the dead of Hiroshima and Nagasaki.
- To remind people of the horrors of nuclear weapons.
- To remind people that nuclear weapons must never be used again.
- A way of saying sorry to the Japanese.
- A reminder to people of the importance of peace.
- To promote the interests of CND.
- To suggest that the war dead died for nothing.

5 FAITH IN THE CITY

YOU WILL BE LOOKING AT TWO CONTRASTING LIFESTYLES, AND THINKING ABOUT HOW PEOPLE LIVING IN THE TOWN AND IN THE COUNTRY CAN SUPPORT EACH OTHER.

THE BOY

Working in pairs, answer the following questions.

1 How old is the boy?

2 What is he doing?

3 What is he waiting for?

4 Where does he live and what is his house like?

5 How does he get on at school?

6 What is his future?

7 If he could plan his future, what would it be like?

8 Think of a name for the boy. Put yourself in his place and write about how you spent the day when this photograph was taken. (You may use ideas you developed in answering questions 1-7.)

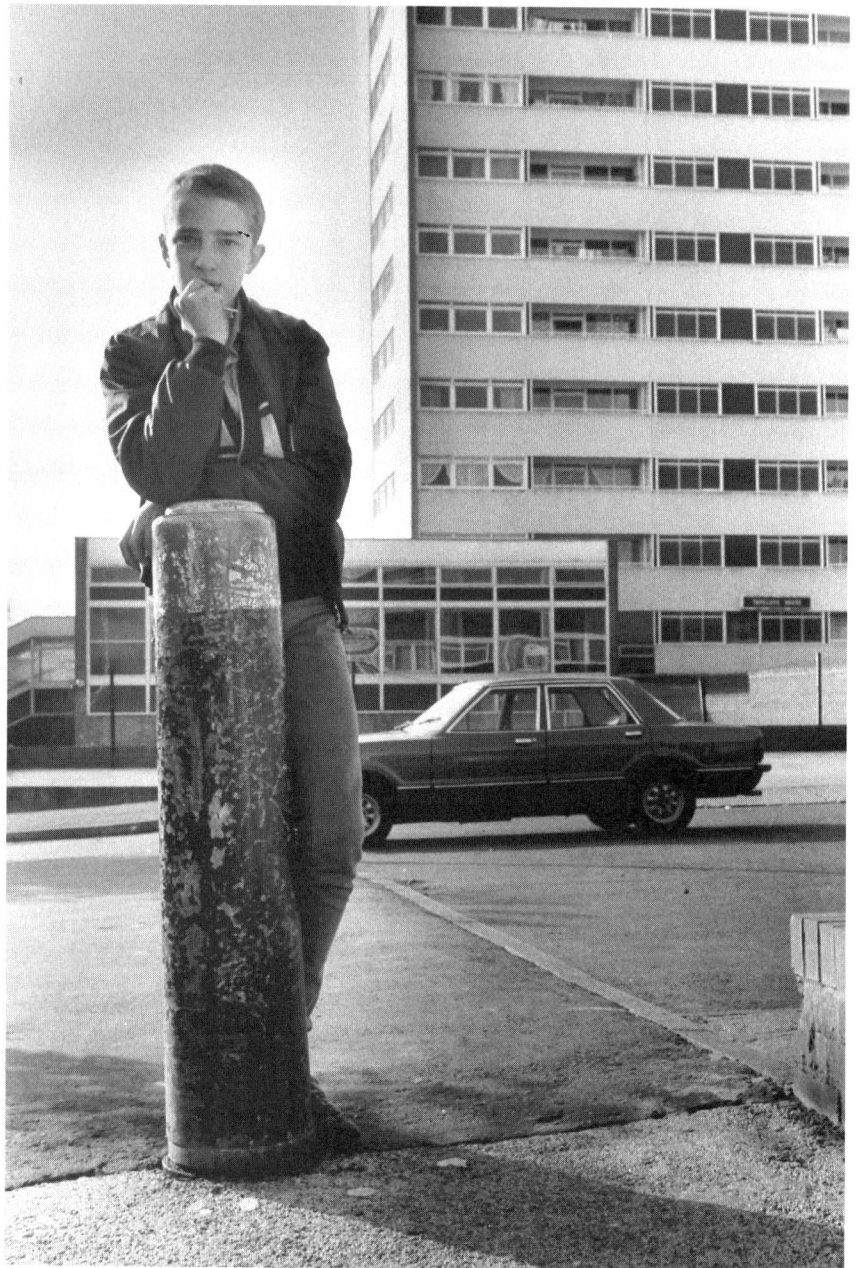

THE CHURCH REPORT

In 1983 the Archbishop of Canterbury, Dr Robert Runcie, appointed a group of people to study the place of the Church in URBAN PRIORITY AREAS (inner cities and large estates with few amenities). The group had to report their findings and make suggestions as to what the Church should be doing in the inner cities. The report was published in a book called *Faith in the City*.

Extract 1

. . . the Church of England has a presence in all the UPAs, and a responsibility to bring their needs to the attention of the nation. If our Report has a distinctive stance, it arises from our determination to investigate the urban situation by bringing to bear upon it those basic Christian principles of justice and compassion *which we believe we share with the great majority of the people of Britain.*

DISCUSS AND WRITE

Read extract 1.
Discuss these questions in small groups with one person taking notes of what the group decides. When you have finished, display your answers and compare them to the answers given by other groups. Notice any similarities and differences between your answers and theirs.

1 '. . . the Church of England has a presence in all the UPAs' [Urban Priority Areas]. What does this mean? List any signs of this presence which you can think of in an inner-city area which you know.

2 What do these words mean?
   justice
   compassion

3 Why do you think 'justice and compassion' are described as Christian principles? (Clue: look up these passages in the Bible – Amos 5:10-13; Luke 4:38-40; Luke 7:18-23.)

4 From your study of religions, would you say that justice and compassion are regarded as important by people of faiths other than Christianity. Give examples.

5 Do you think it is true that most people in Britain feel that 'justice and compassion' are important principles? What evidence do you have to support your answer?

CITY LIFE AND COUNTRY LIFE

Read extract 2 (opposite page). Then do the following activities in groups.

1 Look carefully at the two photographs. Imagine what it must be like to live in these two places. In what ways do you think the lives of the people living in Northchester are:

a) similar   and **b)** different

from the lives of people living in Great Southmead?

List as many similarities and differences as you can.

Living in Northchester

Living in Great Southmead

2 What do you think are the advantages and disadvantages of living in both these places?

3 What indirect contribution could the people living in Northchester be making to the lives of the people living in Great Southmead?

4 What do you understand by 'support' and 'solidarity'?

5 In what ways could the people of Great Southmead show their support for and solidarity with the people living in this part of Northchester?

6 Martin Pelham is the vicar of Great Southmead. After reading the report *Faith in the City*, he decides to have an 'Inner City Awareness Month' at his Church. Suppose that your group is the committee working with him to plan the month. You have been given the following tasks to do. How will you do them? (You could actually carry out your plans in school.)

a) You have to design activities which will make people aware of the problems in the Urban Priority Areas.

b) A number of people in Great Southmead are saying that the problems of the cities are nothing to do with them. You have to persuade them that this is not the case.

c) Having persuaded a number of people in the village that they should be concerned about the inner cities, you have to plan some practical ways in which members of the villages can *show* their concern.

COMMUNITY VALUES

Read extract 3 carefully. Then, in your groups, select one or more of the following activities.

1 *'Community'* has a wide range of meanings. Make two lists. The first list should have the heading 'SMALL GROUPS'. List all the groups to which you belong under the appropriate heading.

2 'The Christian community is local, but part of a wider community, a universal Church.' What do you understand this sentence to mean? Design a poster or card which could be displayed in a church to explain the meaning of the sentence.

3 a) What do you understand by the word 'values'?

b) What are 'material needs'? Are they the same in every community?

c) '...beyond the mere satisfaction of material needs'. What does this phrase mean? What sort of values are important beyond material needs?

Extract 2

We call on Christians throughout this country to listen to the voices of our neighbours who live in the UPAs, to receive the distinctive contribution that they (not least the black people among them) can make to our common life, and to set an example to the nation by making our support of and solidarity with them a high priority in our policies, our actions and our prayers.

Extract 3

Today the word 'community' has a wide range of meanings, denoting anything from a specific group with a warm community spirit to a vague concept of society in general. The Church has a particular understanding of the word. A Christian community is local, but part of a wider community, a universal Church. It is one that is open to and responsible for the whole of society, and which proclaims its care for the weak, its solidarity with all, and its values which lie beyond the mere satisfaction of material needs.

(from the *Faith in the City* report)

A CITY OF MANY FAITHS

Read extract 4. Discuss these questions.

1 What do you understand by the following words or phrases?
consensus   evident dedication   confrontation   spirituality
cultural heritage

2 Explain, in your own words, what the group meant when they reported that Christians should not 'confront' people of other faiths.

3 In what ways does the report suggest that Christians can be of assistance to people of other faiths?

4 There is a small community of Hindus in Northchester. They do not have a temple, and are hoping to buy a church which closed two years ago. However, Christians in Northchester are very divided in their opinions. Some are happy that the Hindu community should buy the Church, but others do not want them to have it.

   Join with another group. One group should take the part of those in favour, and the other group take the part of those against. Plan very carefully the arguments you will use – remember that it is not only members of the Hindu community who are in favour of the sale.

A COMMUNITY MURAL

Here is an example from an inner-city neighbourhood in Peterborough where the community have produced a pleasant, attractive addition to their environment. The people depicted in the mural are real people who live in the area – even the dog is real!

Extract 4

The emphasis on community may also help us to come to terms with the presence in our cities of members of other faiths. There is a growing consensus in the Church of England that confrontation is no longer appropriate for Christians in the face of the evident dedication, spirituality and search for truth shown by so many members of other faiths. Christian service to the community may take the form of helping others to maintain their religious and cultural heritage in freedom and dignity. This may involve the generous use of Church resources, including buildings.

(from the *Faith in the City* report)

Peterborough mural

MAKE YOUR OWN MURAL

How closely do you notice the people around you? In groups, design a mural like the one in Peterborough. But in your mural draw people who live and work in the area around your school.

101 USES OF AN INNER-CITY CHURCH

1 How many different activities are going on here? Note down as many as you can.

2 If you walked up the stairs and into the Church, what do you think you would find going on inside?

3 What message is the cartoonist trying to get across?

4 Might the suggestions made in this cartoon upset some people?
Give reasons for your answer.

MAKING USE OF A DERELICT CHURCH

This church in Northchester is falling down. Money is being donated which will make it possible to turn this derelict building into something which will be of benefit to the local community. The roof and the walls have to be taken down, and there is not enough money to put up a new building.

In your groups, plan what you would do with the site. Also, many of the villagers in Great Southmead have taken an interest in the project. Apart from giving money, how might they be able to help?

YOU WILL BE THINKING ABOUT THE PLACE OF WOMEN IN SOME RELIGIONS TODAY.

What is the message of this poster?

WOMEN IN JUDAISM

What are these women doing?
Look in some RE books for pictures of people doing something similar. How many people in the pictures are women?

Prayer and liturgy

The forming of women's prayer or tefilla groups has mainly served as an alternative for those excluded from active participation in all parts of the synagogue service. Yet all-female groups have often been the most innovative in the area of liturgy. Members have reintroduced techinot (personal prayers composed by East European women in yiddish) and written their own prayers and prayer books.

The study of prayer has led to a discussion of its most fundamental element – language. Descriptions have traditionally identified God with males and 'masculine' attributes as Father, Master, Lord, Ruler and God of our forefathers. Many women feel unable to identify with terminology which ignores them and their experiences. They have proposed several solutions to correct this imbalance:

- The use of neutral or inclusive language whereby Master is replaced by Creator, Lord by Eternal, God of our forefathers by God of our ancestors.
- The inclusion of female images and (pro)nouns as Queen, Mother, Shechina (God's presence), she/her.

The public sphere

Women have generally been excluded from the public sphere. Their testimony is considered unreliable and so they may not serve as witnesses. The functions of rabbi and judge are those of master of Jewish law. Women have traditionally been denied access to the study providing the required knowledge, and authority has rarely been granted to learned women. Despite the ruling that all may called to the Torah, women have been excluded because of the 'honour of the family' i.e. a woman's being called up implies that no man is able. The opening of leadership positions to women is very recent both in the synagogue and in Jewish organisation in general. Conservative Judaism ordained its first woman rabbi in 1985. Many see this as the definitive break with Orthodoxy.

Once married, women are said to be occupied with time-consuming domestic tasks. Consequently, all women have been released from the fulfilling of most positive commandments such as daily prayer, the donning of phylacteries (tefillin) or prayer shawl (tallit). Although not forbidden from doing so, women choosing to fulfil these mitzvot (commandments) are often frowned upon.

FURTHER EXAMPLES

What is this woman doing? Why is this an unusual picture?

Nearly all the major world religions are led by men. Men lead the worship and teach the beliefs of the faith. In Christianity, women cannot be priests in Roman Catholic, Anglican or Orthodox Churches. Women can be Buddhist nuns, but in many places they do not play as important a part as monks. In Islam and Orthodox Judaism, the commands to say formal prayers each day do not apply to women, only to men. More and more women of all faiths are finding this state of affairs unacceptable. Some changes have been made. In Reform, Conservative and Liberal Judaism, women can be rabbis, and in Protestant Churches women may be ministers.

RESEARCH

1 Find out what the objections are against women becoming priests. Discuss these reasons, and say whether or not you agree with them.

2 Collect as many examples as you can of women (of any faith) who have played an important role in religion. Make a display of your research.

▷▷▷ RE-WRITING 'HE' AND 'HIS'

'23'

She is my guide so I need nothing more
She makes me lie down in green pastures
She leads me beside still waters
She restores my soul
She leads me in the paths of wholeness, the paths she creates.
Even though I'm scared of the dark I know no fear
For she is with me
Her strength and her courage they comfort me.
She encourages me to approach those people I don't understand
And when she shows me her way
Then I do understand
I hope her example will be with me all the days of my life
And I shall dwell in her light for ever.

(from *Bringing the Invisible into the Light*)

Compare this psalm to the original Psalm 23 in the Bible. Talk about what you think and feel about the changes.
Find another well-known prayer or song and re-write it twice:
a) the first time, make the references to God female;
b) the second time, replace words which suggest that God is male or female with words that do not suggest either sex. Discuss which of the three versions you prefer.
c) In your groups, write down the qualities of God as you see them. Which of these qualities need to be either male or female qualities?

▷▷▷ DISCUSSION

1 From your reading of all the texts, list the things which women are complaining about. What complaints do these women of different faiths have in common?

2 What similar ideas are expressed in '23' and 'Prayer and liturgy' (page 25)?

3 Why do you think God has always been described in masculine terms?

4 Many women say that they are not able to identify with a god who is described totally in masculine terms. Why do you think this is?

5 Why do you think that in most major religions women are still prevented from playing a leading role?

7 IN PRISON

YOU WILL BE THINKING ABOUT WHAT IT WOULD BE LIKE TO BE DEPRIVED OF HUMAN RIGHTS – ABOUT WHY THERE ARE PRISONERS OF CONSCIENCE, WHY AND HOW SOME PEOPLE SUPPORT THEM.

PRISONERS OF CONSCIENCE

Amnesty International is an organisation which works for the release of *prisoners of conscience*. These are people who have been imprisoned because they are known to hold beliefs which the Government of their country find dangerous. Most of the prisoners supported by Amnesty have done nothing more than join in demonstrations, or speak out against their Government.

Many countries in the world detain prisoners on the basis of their beliefs alone. One such country is Chile. In 1973 there was a military coup in Chile. Since then there have been no political parties and no elections. The Church is almost the only organised body left which can voice the views of the people who do not agree with the military government. Many people, including students and church leaders, have been imprisoned and tortured – in some cases, killed – for speaking out against the Government.

Amnesty International

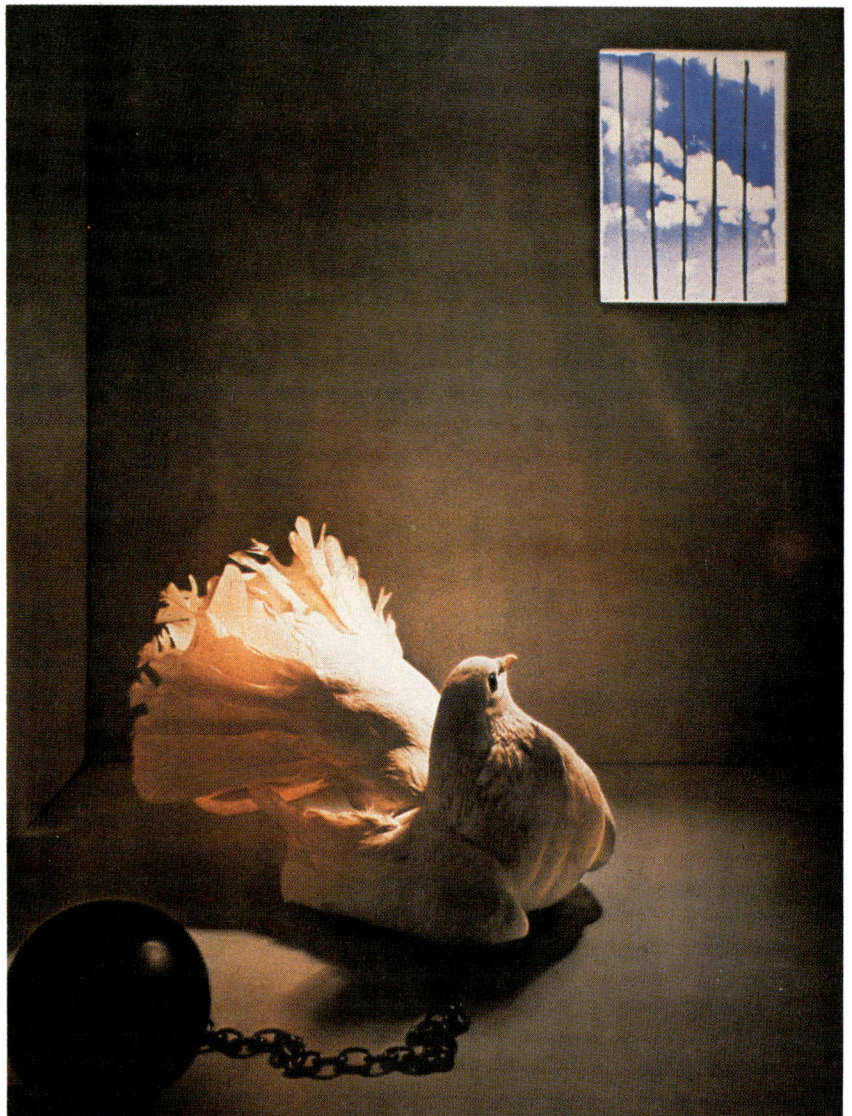

28

PRISONER BEFRIENDING SCHEMES

There are a number of organisations in Britain which 'adopt' prisoners of conscience: they include the Prisoner Befriending Scheme (Quaker) and Action by Christians against Torture (British Council of Churches). People who support these schemes adopt one prisoner, write regular letters to him or her, send Christmas cards, and sometimes write to their Government and to the United Nations (UN) requesting their release.

The Quaker group alone noted the following figures for 1987:

Prisoners befriended: 100   Released: 34
(Chile: 50; Argentina: 37; Indonesia: 8; USSR: 5)
Replied (prisoner or contact): 60   Known to have been tortured: 33

This tapestry illustrates the United Nations declaration: **EVERYONE HAS THE RIGHT TO FREEDOM OF PEACEFUL ASSEMBLY.**

Design (and make if you have the time) a tapestry to illustrate the article below from the UN Declaration of Human Rights.

Article 18 says:

'Everyone has the right to freedom of thought, conscience and religion; this right includes freedom to change his [or her] religion or belief, and freedom, either alone or in community with others and in public or in private, to manifest his [or her] religion or belief in teaching, practice, worship and observance.'

When a card is a lifeline

The Prisoner Befriending Scheme is probably by now well known to Friends, especially when at this time of year Christmas card lists are sent out so that individuals and Meetings can send greetings to political prisoners. The Scheme continues all year; lifelines are cast towards prisoners and their families in the form of letters of support, and from time to time the joyful news of a release gives encouragement to those who are patiently writing while sometimes there is little hope of a reply. One such prisoner, Leonardo Saavedra, who was befriended by Peter Dyson, is now at liberty and recently spoke in London of his ordeal in Chile to Friends attending the Yearly Meeting.

'They don't need any excuse for arresting people; it's enough to be known to hold opinions against government policy. The charge against me was that I had been organising paramilitary groups among my fellow-students, but not a scrap of evidence was produced. They often just assume that students are subversive. They are afraid of students and others with education, who are articulate; that is their fear – that people can express their views – so they try to link such people with a charge of violence so as to justify their imprisonment.

'The most terrible time for me was after I had arrived at the Security Police headquarters, when I was interrogated. They are really experts in torture. One of the most usual methods is electric shocks. In repeated sessions they put me in different positions and applied electric shocks all over my body. The worst was when they trussed me up like a chicken, hanging from a bar and, when I was helpless, they applied electricity to my testicles, anus and all the most sensitive parts. At the same time they asked me everything they could think of, in order to find out how much I knew.

'After the interrogations I was put into solitary confinement for 10 days. The cell was two square metres. There was no bed but in the early hours of the morning they threw in a bundle of rags for me to sleep on. Then, in the detention cell for the next two years,

This photograph of Leonardo in prison in Chile was smuggled out and received by Great Bardfield Friends.

everything was done to degrade me. The food was revolting and there was nothing to eat it with but my fingers. I was subjected to constant harassment, like being woken up at 3 a.m. while a big search was made of my cell, even though there was nothing to find.

'Even after my release I had to report to the police station every fortnight for a year. Ex-prisoners are not left in peace. We were

always looking over our shoulders, afraid of being re-arrested.

'We ex-prisoners were frustrated. We were young, concerned people; students. We still wanted to do something to improve the economic situation of our country. This is what had got us into prison. Eventually I decided it was better to leave the country than to be useless.'

Peter Dyson adds: 'I didn't want to listen to the details. I had to make myself listen. It bothers me that I too want to hide it and pretend it isn't there, but he needed to share it and we needed to know – to know and confront. It still exists and we still have to abolish it, but in the meantime we must care for its victims.

'Leonardo did not dwell on his sufferings – they were but a small part of a total life and it was the whole that my Meeting sought to befriend.'

The last word belongs to Leonardo: 'It is enormously important to those in prison to know there are people far away who are concerned about them and who write to them. It is a great excitement to get a card at Christmas. All this is absolutely wonderful and is something that really keeps prisoners going in their sufferings. I want to thank everyone who writes to prisoners and I hope there will be more people doing this because it is a real support to those still in the conditions I have been through.'

1 What attitudes and activities led to Leonardo being arrested?

2 All over the world, students often take part in demonstrations for or against various causes. Why do you think this is?

3 What are the main political differences between governments which do allow freedom of belief and those which do not?

4 Why do you think some governments are afraid of people who speak against them?

5 Measure out a square two metres by two metres. What would you imagine to be the major problems of being in solitary confinement for 10 days? What would you do to try to cope if it happened to you?

6 What do you think the police were trying to achieve by torturing and humiliating Leonardo?

7 Write a letter to Leonardo in prison. You will need to discuss carefully the sort of letter he will want to receive.

IF . . .

1 In Britain people are free to express their views about the government of the day.
   a) How many ways can you think of by which people express those views?
   b) How might the Government deal with criticism by people
      i) who are opposed to them?
      ii) who are supposed to be on their side?

2 Imagine that yesterday one party, or the armed forces or the police force, took control of Britain. All opposition to the new government is banned.
   a) Write down all the changes which you think would take place.
   b) Re-write a day in your life (perhaps today or yesterday) under these conditions. (NB Think of the differences in school, with friends in the street, television, newspapers, music.)

RESEARCH

Find out all you can about Nelson and Winnie Mandela. Why are so many people in the world supporting them, and why has the South African Government been so opposed to them?

Why should torture be a crime against God?

> **Torture is a Crime against God and Humanity**

Winnie Mandela

*YOU WILL BE THINKING ABOUT THE STRESSES OF
MODERN LIFE AND HOW PEOPLE TRY TO
HELP OTHER PEOPLE OVERCOME THEM.*

The notices shown opposite tell us a lot about the human problems faced by many people.

SUPPORT GROUPS

1 Draw two columns on a piece of paper. Head one column 'GROUP' and the other 'PROBLEM'. List the names of all the groups in the one column and in the other make a note of the problem which that group seeks to help solve. What sort of problems seem to be most widespread?

Red Balloon

2 a) Unmarried mothers are not the only one-parent families. What other groups of people constitute one-parent families?

b) Why do you think it may be helpful for one-parent families to meet together? What problems might they have in common?

c) If you were a single parent attending the Red Balloon group, what 'information and advice' do you think you might be looking for?

VOLUNTARY WORK

1 Look at the advertisement for voluntary workers. If you were to volunteer to work a few hours a week, what sort of activities do you think you would be doing?

2 Do this exercise with a friend. If you were to volunteer to help with one of the groups,
a) which one would you most like to work with?
b) what qualities do you think you have which would make you a valuable addition to that particular group?
Do you and your friend agree as to what qualities you each have?

RESEARCH

See how many similar notices you can find for groups in your area. You may find information in church magazines, town halls, citizens' advice bureaux, public libraries etc. Make a display of what you find out.

9 DOWN AND OUT

YOU WILL BE THINKING ABOUT HOMELESSNESS AND SOME OF ITS CAUSES – AND HOW AND WHY PEOPLE TRY TO HELP THE HOMELESS. YOU WILL ALSO BE THINKING ABOUT YOUR OWN AND OTHER PEOPLE'S ATTITUDES TO THE HOMELESS.

A ROOF OVER THEIR HEADS

Extract 1

Planning refusal for hostel costs charity £33,500 extra

A charity whose attempts to buy a £68,000 Bury St Edmunds property for a homeless hostel were thwarted, has now purchased it nearly 12 months later at a cost of £101,501.

The Stonham Housing Association's consultant architect, Mr Philip Woods, confirmed yesterday that the association had bought the former Britannia pub, Ipswich Street, to be run by the charity, the Cyrenians. The housing association will convert the former pub into accommodation for 10 single homeless people. Mr Woods said they hoped it would be ready by this time next year.

Work is due to start in the spring on renovating the run-down property which was purchased through estate agents Prudential from Sam Construction, a local property consortium.

The Cyrenians wanted to buy the property for £68,000 less than 12 months ago from brewer Greene King, but planning consent was refused. It was given the go-ahead on appeal, but by then the property had been sold to Sam Construction, which gained planning permission for flats.

Mrs Joan Hobson, local Cyrenians' secretary, said the need for accommodation for single homeless people had greatly increased since the search for a property began some four years ago.

The hostel's residents will contribute to its running costs, but further money will have to be raised to pay staff. An estimated £100,000 will be spent on refurbishing the property.

One volunteer worker for the homeless described the sale profit as 'disgusting'. Nothing has apparently been done to the property since the original purchase and it was now more dilapidated, she said.

Read extracts 1 and 2.

1 a) Why do you think a charity for helping the homeless should call itself the 'Cyrenians'? (Clue: see Luke 23:26.)

   b) Try to find out the name of another charity for the homeless which took its name from the same person.

Extract 2

Shelter for Christmas opened

A last-minute offer made this week means homeless people in Bury St Edmunds will have a roof over their heads this Christmas.

The Lathbury Institute in Church Row has become vacant and Rev Simon Pettitt of St John's Church has offered the building as a shelter until March. The news came as a relief to Shelter at Christmas, the organisation founded in 1986 to help the homeless through the cold months. Originally its committee – drawn from organisations all over the town – had enlisted the help of churches to provide accommodation for a fortnight at a time.

Rev Pettitt said although people had responded generously with offers of help most churches would have found it very inconvenient to convert their halls into a shelter each night.

'We don't know yet how many people are likely to take advantage of the shelter but I know of one man already who is sleeping rough and just waiting for it to open.'

Shelter at Christmas chairperson Julia Wakelam welcomed the offer of the institute and said it would provide a temporary solution to a growing problem of homelessness in Bury St Edmunds.

'Many people do not fit into categories which must be legally housed by the council. The cost of accommodation in town is so high they are left with nowhere to live. It is a problem we hope will eventually be solved by permanent premises for the homeless.'

Those using the shelter will be given bedclothes and a

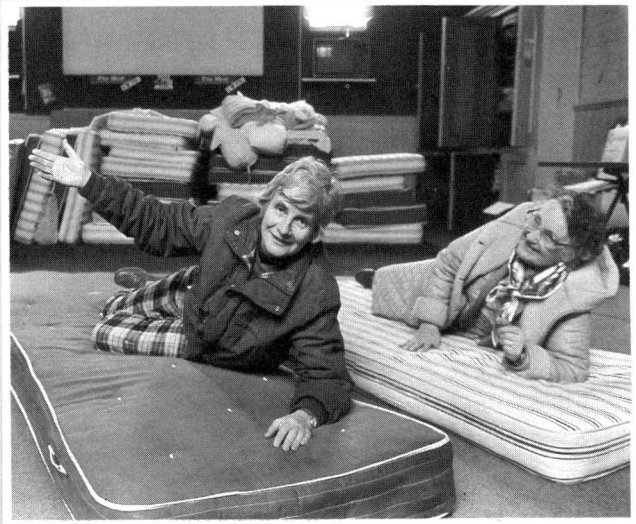

Shelter at Christmas . . . Elizabeth Gatland and Joan Hobson inside the Lathbury Institute in Bury St Edmunds

mattress, and a shower has been supplied. Food is available morning and evening.

Volunteers are mainly drawn from churches of all denominations.

The venture has received £700 from Suffolk County Council's chairman's fund and is to get £500 from St Edmundsbury Borough Council.

Ms Julia Rynard, group chairwoman, said the shelter's users were people who, through no fault of their own, could not find anywhere to live. It was wrong to think homeless people were to blame for their situation, she added.

---

2 Why could the Cyrenians not buy the Britannia at a lower price a year earlier?

3 Who gives planning permission, and what is the procedure for getting it? Why do you think Sam Construction got planning permission for converting the pub into flats, whereas the Cyrenians had found it very difficult?

4 How much profit did Sam Construction make on the deal?

5 One volunteer said that the profit made on the deal was 'disgusting'. What did she mean? Give reasons for agreeing or disagreeing with her.

6 Suggest reasons why people become homeless.

7 When people become homeless, what else are they likely to lose apart from their home?

8 If the Church Row shelter had not opened for the Christmas period, how do you think the visitors there would have spent Christmas?

9 Imagine that you are one of the people waiting for accommodation in the Britannia. Write a letter to the newspaper giving an account of a day in your life in winter, and explaining why you need the accommodation.

10 Why do you think the Churches are interested in supporting the venture?

GROUP ACTIVITY

Collect information from people in your class who are familiar with a church hall. In your groups, design a 'typical' church hall using the information you have collected.

Now your group is about to become the 'church hall committee'. You will need to elect a chairperson, secretary and treasurer. You have £150 in the kitty.

It has just been decided that your hall is to become an overnight shelter for the homeless over the Christmas period. You have *two weeks* to make your preparations. You will need to consider the following:

- staffing
- safety precaution
- money
- food
- facilities
- rules.

Use one lesson for a planning meeting to decide on exactly what has to be done. Divide the jobs between members of the group. Try to plan the activity as though you were really doing it. What are the biggest problems?

After two weeks, present your plan to the whole class, and show what you have been able to do.

Would you like to spend Christmas doing this sort of thing 'in real life'?

SURVEY

Find out what people feel about the homeless.
Whose fault is it?
Who is responsible for housing the homeless?
What other questions will you need to ask if you want to find out about people's attitudes towards homelessness?

THE PORCH

What is the 'Porch'?

The Porch is a small refreshment centre where tea and sandwiches are provided free of charge at specified hours of the day. It is also a place where useful information can be exchanged on such subjects as medical services, legal advice, and financial benefits, and where the company of others can be enjoyed.

How did it begin?

For some years the Sisters at All Saints Convent provided refreshments for those who came to their door asking for something to eat. The callers were usually unemployed and many of them homeless. The porch at the front door had begun to seem inhospitable and inadequate, providing only minimal shelter, and the number of callers was increasing rapidly; so in the autumn of 1986 part of a building in the convent grounds was adapted to become the new 'Porch'. The callers were involved with the small voluntary committee of people associated with the Society of All Saints in planning the centre and in considering the rules required, in raising funds for the project and in the training of voluntary helpers.

Who does it serve?

The Porch welcomes old friends and new, anyone in need of a cup of tea and a sandwich, warmth and hospitality. There is room for up to 25 people at any one time and it is open for several hours each day, morning and evening. Alcohol and drugs are not allowed on the premises and no money is exchanged.

Who serves in the Porch?

Volunteers are drawn from the Society of All Saints, its Associates and friends; from students who undertake the service as a project during their training for Church ministry or social service; from those living in the neighbourhood.

What costs are involved?

Building work, decorating, furnishing and equipping the Porch is costing £14,000 which has been raised thanks to the generosity of individuals and groups locally and through interest-free loans. The Society does not charge rent, and maintenance work, cleaning and serving are all undertaken by volunteers.

Running costs are:
£20 a week for food
£4 a week for heat and light.

Callers

So far the Porch seems to have three main groups of callers: people who are sleeping out or on Night Shelter, or are in bed and breakfast type accommodation; people who have been in hospital after a breakdown and may now be in halfway houses; younger people who use Night Cellar. But this is just a surface view. Our callers are much more important as *who* they are than as *what* they are. We learn about each other every day. Expectations of the Porch vary, but those who helped to plan the Porch when they served tea at the front door of the convent wanted a QUIET, friendly place where they could be for just a little while.

Read all the extracts.

GROUP WORK

1   What have you found out about
    a) the people who work at the Porch (the volunteers)?
    b) the people who call at the Porch (the callers)?

2   Why do the callers go to the Porch?

3   When the Porch was designed, callers as well as the committee were involved in
    planning the building, making the rules, and fundraising.
    a) Why do you think the callers were involved?
    b) Do you think this was a good idea?

4   Why do you think the following rules were made?
    ■ No alcohol or drugs to be taken into the Porch.
    ■ No money to be exchanged.

5   Find words or phrases in the extract which tell you something about the attitude
    of the people who work at the Porch towards the callers. Write a short summary
    of what you have discovered. What words would *you* use to describe their
    attitude?

6   People who have no home and no money often call at Convents and Vicarages
    asking for something to eat and drink. Why do you think they call at these places
    rather than private homes?

7   a) Why do you think Christians are concerned for the poor and the homeless?
        (Clue: Matthew 25:31-44)
    b) Do you know, or can you find out about, ways in which people of other
        religious faiths support the poor?

8   The Porch is open during mornings and evenings. How do you think the callers
    spend the rest of the day, and where might they go at night?

9   Students training to be priests, ministers and social workers are among the
    volunteers at the Porch.
    a) What sort of work do you think they do?
    b) In what ways might this be valuable experience for them?

10 The community is asking for contributions to help run the Porch.
    a) Is this a charity you feel you would like to support? Give your reasons.
    b) If you were to support it, which of the ways of helping suggested in the
        information would you prefer to adopt? Say why.

11 If someone decides to give money to a charity, explain why giving a covenant is
    more helpful to the charity than a cash donation.

CREATIVE WORK

1 Design a large poster telling people about the Porch. In your poster, try to express the *attitude* of the community.

2 Write a poem with the title 'The Porch People'.

ATTITUDES

'You won't catch me giving money to these charities for the homeless. They got themselves into the mess – they can get themselves out of it.'

'I think it's totally wrong that charities for the homeless should exist at all. It's the job of the Government and local authorities to house people. They are just taking advantage of people's good nature.'

'Being able to show our love and care for people worse off than ourselves is one of the few ways left to us in this day and age for showing our humanity. The existence of voluntary caring organisations is one of the few signs left of what human beings should be – one of the few reminders to us of how fortunate we are. Through them we have an opportunity to show our gratitude for all that we have.'

'I'm more interested in changing the society which gives rise to such hardship. I'd rather spend my time bringing about long-term change for everyone than making life comfortable for a few homeless people once or twice a week.'

WHAT DO YOU THINK????????

10 ENVIRONMENT

*YOU WILL BE THINKING ABOUT THE PLANET WE LIVE ON –
WHAT IT IS LIKE, HOW WE TREAT IT, AND HOW WE FEEL ABOUT IT.
ALSO YOU WILL BE LOOKING AT IDEAS ABOUT BALANCE
IN THE UNIVERSE, AND THE RELATION OF HUMAN BEINGS
TO THE PLANET.*

PLANET FOR SALE

A prospective purchaser has made an offer for this delightful detached residence. As is normal with property purchases, they have hired a surveyor to make a report on the property. If you were the surveyor, what points would you make in your report on the property under the following headings?

GOOD POINTS
BAD POINTS
WORK TO BE DONE IN THE NEAR FUTURE BEFORE YOUR CLIENT COULD LIVE IN IT

MAN ON THE MOON

When James Irwin stood on the Moon and looked out at the Earth, he described it as looking 'fragile', and 'like a Christmas tree decoration' hanging in space. What feelings do you get when you see pictures and films of the Earth taken from space?

Many people say that such a beautifully designed system must have a designer. What do you say?

MAINTAINING THE BALANCE

This is the Chinese symbol for Yin and Yang. In Chinese philosophy there are two forces in the universe which are very carefully balanced. Yang is a positive, active force. It stands for:

WARM   HARD   DRY   BRIGHT   STEADFAST.

Yin is a negative, passive force. It stands for:

COLD   WET   DARK   MYSTERIOUS   SECRET   CHANGING.

There is a Yin and Yang in all things, and the balance between them may change from time to time. They are not in conflict, but in harmony. What keeps the balance between the two forces is Tao, the way of nature, the law of life. This balance can be illustrated by fire and water. If there was all fire and no water there would be total destruction. If there was all water and no heat to evaporate it, there would again be total destruction. It is when humans interfere with the system of Tao that chaos results and the balance of the universe is disturbed.

ACTIVITY

Draw a set of scales with Tao at the apex holding the balance between Yin in one balance and Yang in the other. List or draw under Yin and Yang the opposite but balancing forces (e.g. light and darkness) which you think belong to each heading.

GREENPEACE

Greenpeace is an organisation which is concerned with the care of the planet. In this collage of extracts from a Greenpeace leaflet you can see some of the problems which Greenpeace is concerned about.

GREEN POLITICS - THE FACTS

Planet in peril

Green activists hold that the quick-profit approach of industrial decision-makers is creating a world that will be uninhabitable for future generations. Evidence is mounting that the Greens are right. NI takes stock of the growing threat to our lives and livelihood.

Failing water tables

Though yearly rainfall remains fairly constant, the world's use of water is doubling every ten to twenty years. As a result the water table – the depth at which you will find water underground – is steadily falling.[3]

● In the south Indian state of Tamil Nadu irrigation is lowering the water table by one to four metres a year.
● In the US, irrigated land decreased by 3% in the 1978-83 period. Parts of the giant Ogallala water basin under the Great Plains are at least half depleted.

Disappearing forests

The world's forest resource is quickly being depleted by lumber companies – or by those trying to keep warm or cook their food. The problem is particularly severe in the Third World where much more forest land is being cleared than planted.[5]

Trees cleared to trees re-planted

Africa	29 to 1
Latin America	10 to 1
Asia	5 to 1

Plundered resources

Soil loss

A third of the world's people live in countries where cropland is shrinking. Topsoil is being lost due to overcultivation, improper irrigation, ploughed grassland, and deforestation. In Africa the Sahara desert gobbles up 30 miles a year in its relentless march southwards.[1]

Country	Loss per acre (tons)
US	7
USSR	4
India	14
China	13
Rest of the world	6

Shrinking fish stocks

One of the major sources of protein – the world's fish catch – is beginning to show signs of wear.[4]

Growth in world fish catch

Period	Total	Per capita
1950 – 1970	5.9%	3.8%
1970 – 1983	1.0%	-0.8%

Fouled air

The three main sources of air pollution are industry, energy production and the automobile.

A 1,000 megawatt power plant burning coal that gives off smoke containing 10% ash, 1.5% sulphur, and 1.5% nitrogen will produce per hour:

900 tons of carbon dioxide
12 tons of sulphur compounds
5 tons of nitric acid
3 to 5 tons of soot particles
30 tons of ash[6]

Smog

Severe urban air pollution or smog causes respiratory problems in people and plants. There is high daily variance in urban smog density.

Sulphur Dioxide (milligrams per cubic metre)[7]

City	Maximum*	Average
Milan (Italy)	1,641	353
Brussels (Belgium)	614	96
Madrid (Spain)	605	102
São Paulo (Brazil)	483	153
Santiago (Chile)	320	137

*US air quality standard is 80 milligrams.

Acid rain

Many lakes in North America and Europe receive up to 30 times more acidity than they would if rain and snow fell through clean air.

Percentage of West German forests damaged by acid rain*

1982	1983	1984
8%	34%	50%

● In Canada 14,000 lakes are dead. Some 40,000 more are dying. Also 90 of Ontario sugar maples in a 20,000 sq. kilometre area are dying. In the province of Quebec 14% of sugar maple trees are already dead.[9]
● Current trends suggest that atmospheric pollutants and acidity in precipitation will increase in much of the industrial and developing world.[10]

Climate in crisis

The waste products of industrial society are beginning to threaten the global climate.

Greenhouse effect

Accumulated pollutants in the atmosphere – primarily carbon dioxide, methane and chlorofluorocarbons – are blocking solar heat rays that normally travel back into space. This is causing global temperatures to rise. By early in the next century the global temperature could be higher than any time in the last 100,000 years. This would alter growing seasons and cause the polar ice caps partially to melt. Sea levels may rise by as much as three feet by the year 2050 causing flooding in low lying areas.[11]

Ozone layer depletion

Ozone protects life on earth from ultra-violet radiation given off by the sun. The ozone layer is gradually being broken down by 655,000 tons of chlorofluorocarbons released by industry every year. US scientists report a 30% reduction of the ozone layer over the Antarctic. The US Environmental Protection Agency estimates that a 2.5% reduction in the ozone layer could cause 15,000 human cancers per year as well as extensive damage to crops.[13]

Radiation damage

Fall-out continues from nuclear bomb tests that took place in the 1950s and 1960s. And there have been nuclear power reactor accidents at Three Mile Island and in Chernobyl where 29 people died from exposure to high levels of radiation. The Swedish Academy of Sciences estimates up to 8,000 European cancers will be caused by Chernobyl.

Fragile ecosystems

Tropical rainforests

These are complex ecosystems with a large diversity of plant and animal life. They are important in maintaining global oxygen levels.
Threat: The destruction of the rainforests is being engineering for the creation of more grazing acreage, for fuel, for roads and military installations, and in order to build a monocrop fast-growth forestry industry. By 1986 tropical forests were disappearing at the rate of 68 million acres a year.[14]

The Arctic regions

The Arctic possesses a very fragile ecosystem with slow decomposition of wastes and thin acidic soil. Precipitation falls in desert-like quantities. There is little species diversity – of 30,000 types of fish only 50 live in the Arctic. Large populations of few species (caribou, seals) are very vulnerable to environmental stress. The Arctic and Antarctic regions play an important role in cooling the earth's climate.[15]
Threat: The Arctic is threatened by potential oil spills in the Beaufort Sea and other Arctic areas where drilling is currently underway. There are also substantial oil reserves in the Antarctic. Oil and gas pipelines in areas such as Canada's Mackenzie Valley disrupt caribou migration patterns and native trapping economies. Military installations and air strips in Canada, the US and the USSR are also a threat and military activity will increase if US Star Wars plans go ahead.

Poisoning the water

Today much of our water is contaminated. Most contaminants become more concentrated and dangerous as they move up the food chain. For example, 1/50 of a part per million of a chemical insecticide in lake water becomes 1,600 parts per million in fish-eating birds.[16]

Water pollution sources:

Domestic sewage is dumped into lagoons, onto land, into rivers and into the sea. In Canada 270 chemical pollutants pass through Ontario sewage treatment plants into Lake Ontario.[17]

Toxic chemicals are sprayed on farms, fields and forests. They run off into streams and lakes and seep through the soil into groundwater.

Industrial wastes include synthetic chemicals and heavy metals that are poured into rivers and lakes and dumped into landfill sites such as Love Canal near Niagara Falls, New York. There are thousands of toxic landfill sites across the industrial world. It is impossible to estimate how many are leaking into ground and surface water.

Oil and chemical spills such as the highly- publicized spill of toxic chemicals into the Rhine river in 1986 or the Torrey Canyon oil spill into the Atlantic in 1967 are just the tip of the iceberg.

Radioactive particles are part of the waste-stream of reactors and some hospitals, and are a contributing factor to human cancers.

Toxins in drinking water

A worldwide survey of drinking water found among the 1,600 chemicals detected:

Recognized carcinogens (cause cancer)	22
Suspected carcinogens	42
Tumor promoters/co-carcinogens	27
Recognized mutagens (cause birth defects)	50
Suspected mutagens	15[18]

1 The Nature of Things, CBC, Toronto, 1986. 2 State of the World, Worldwatch Institute, Washington, 1985. 3 Ibid 4 Ibid 5 Ibid 6 Appleman. Epitaph for Planet Earth, Frederick Fell Publishers Inc. 1982. NY. 7 World Health Organization, Air Quality in Selected Urban Areas 1979 – 80, Geneva 1983. 8 Ibid. 9 Micheal Keating, Globe and Mail, Oct 3rd 1986. 10 Ibid. 11 Macleans June 30 198 12 Ibid. 13 Globe and Mail, May 6 1986. 14 State of the World Report, Worldwatch Institute, 1986, Washington. 15 Barry Lope Arctic Dreams, Doubleday, New York, 1986. 16 Rachel Carson, The Silent Spring, Houghton Mifflin, NY 1962. 17 Pollution Prot Toronto, Ont. 1985. 18 JC Kraybill, Alternatives Magazine, Waterloo, Ont.

Looking at the extracts, list the ways in which Greenpeace sees humanity as interfering with the balance in the universe. Add any other suggestions of your own.

CARE OF THE PLANET

Here are some of the thoughts people have had about the planet on which they live:

'The world has enough for everyone's needs, but not for everyone's greed.'

'Treat the Earth well. It was given to you by your parents. It was loaned to you by your children.'

'The Earth does not belong to man. Man belongs to the Earth.'

▷▷▷ Do you agree with these statements? Give reasons for your answers.

▷▷▷
DISPLAY WORK

Draw or paint a picture which illustrates the idea that the world is 'a mirror of infinite beauty' and 'a region of light and peace'. Or you can make a collage to illustrate the theme. Or find a painting or photograph which you think illustrates these sayings. Make a display of all your pictures and mount a copy of the Traherne poem in the centre.

The world is a mirror of infinite beauty, yet no man regards it. It is a region of light and peace, did not man disquiet it? It is the paradise of God.

(Thomas Traherne)

GRAFFITI BOARD

If I am despairing of myself, I despair of the world's future;
If I am unhopeful of myself, I have no hope for the world;
If I am uncaring for myself, I am careless of my environment and of my sister creatures;
If I am loving, I see the world as cooperative and caring;
If I feel helpless, I see the world at the mercy of events;
If I feel empowered, I see myself making a difference to my friends and my environment;
The outer world acts as a mirror to my inner world.

(from *Inner Ecology* by Stanley Parker)

Write out the above poem on a poster but leave out the last line. Anyone can add lines of their own in the style of the poem, beginning 'If I am . . .' or 'If I feel . . .'. Each line should reflect the idea that our inner feelings affect the way in which we behave . towards others and the environment.

GCSE NOTES FOR THE TEACHER

The three books in this series have been written specifically for use in Religious Education, but they will also be an invaluable resource for teachers of Integrated Humanities, PSE and sixth form general studies. The books are marked by **three fundamental characteristics**:

OPEN-ENDED AND FLEXIBLE

You will find that they can cover each unit in brief in as little time as two weeks, or in depth and by adding ideas of your own in as much as half a term. There is no assumption made that all pupils will engage in all activities, and in fact the books were not designed to be 'text books' to be followed through from beginning to end. Rather, these materials might become 'dippers' to which pupils can turn in the course of their studies to extend their skills and abilities. Most pupils can attempt most of the work in the books. The assignments and activities have been compiled especially to enable pupils of different ages and abilities to respond at their own level.

LEARNING BY THINKING

The books have not been written to convey knowledge of facts. The books are ACTIVITY books, for those lessons where teacher input will be at a minimum, with pupil involvement taking a high profile – the teacher acting in an advisory capacity. It is hoped that teachers will use this material in conjunction with a unit of work on a related topic, and that pupils will work at the activities with a certain amount of knowledge gleaned from elsewhere.

The advent of GCSE has placed greater demand on UNDERSTANDING and EVALUATIVE skills. Many teachers are looking for material which will develop these abilities in years 2 – 5, and this series will meet this need. A number of activities in these books may prove useful as the basis of coursework assignments and have been labelled with this symbol: **KUE** – knowledge, understanding and evaluation.

GCSE ASSESSMENT OBJECTIVES

The National Criteria for Religious Studies do not at present answer the question 'What must candidates be able to DO in order to demonstrate ability in the areas of understanding and evaluation?' Teachers who have puzzled over this in the setting of appropriate coursework may have reached some of the following conclusions:

- Abilities demonstrative of **understanding** involve offering explanations as a result of following through certan processes:
  a) ANALYSIS – this involves breaking down an overall mass of evidence into its constituent elements and where necessary re-constituting elements by means of classification;
  b) INTERPRETATION – ascribing meaning and significance – this skill is particularly appropriate to Religious Education;
  c) APPLICATION – being able to supply what is known to particular circumstances;
  d) EMPATHY – the ability to differentiate one's own response from that of others, and to appreciate the differences between one's own values, beliefs etc. and those of others.

- EVALUATION is largely a matter of *making a personal judgement/response*. Pupils are expected to weigh up arguments using the appropriate evidence, and to give convincing reasons for their own point of view.

GCSE – THE FIELD OF STUDY

These books concentrate on the areas of study common to all syllabuses and currently prescribed by the National Criteria under the heading of **UNDERSTANDING** (see Assessment Objectives 3.2.1 – 3.2.5). These areas of study may be summarised as follows:

Candidates should demonstrate knowledge and understanding of:
a) the language, terms and concepts of religion;
b) the concept of AUTHORITY enshrined in sacred texts, special people, and the traditions of religions;
c) the principal BELIEFS of the religions studied;
d) MORALITY – religious and non-religious responses to contemporary moral issues, both personal and social;
e) ULTIMATE QUESTIONS – identification of those questions beyond which no further questions are possible, and a consideration of selected responses to those questions.

Underlying these categories is a sixth – that of EXPRESSION – the means by which belief is expressed through language, story, symbol, art, music, literature, ritual etc.

HOW DO THESE BOOKS FIT IN WITH GCSE?

Book 1: What Do You Think?

. . . is mainly concerned with looking at moral issues and how they are resolved, and especially with the question of the relationship between belief and behaviour.

Book 2: Life, the Universe and You

. . . explores some of the key questions encountered in life, and in particular looks at the ways in which different people find meaning and purpose in life.

Book 3: Ways of Saying

. . . explores:

- some of the ways in which people experience the presence of what they may (or may not) call God;
- some of the ways in which people, and particularly some religious faiths, have expressed their beliefs and experiences through art, music, architecture, poetry etc.

RESOURCE LISTS

As units will be used within the context of work on a given theme, a list of recommended resources for each unit is given on the next page. Teachers and pupils should also be looking for other stimulus materials in newspapers, magazines etc.

RESOURCES

You will find the books listed here will give you more information on the themes explored in the book. There are also organisations who will send you information if you write to them. Remember you should always enclose a stamped addressed envelope.

1 Credo

The Voice of One Crying in the Wilderness by Desmond Tutu, (ed Webster) Mowbray, 1982
Strength to Love by Martin Luther King, Fontana, 1969
Tape of speech available from CAFOD, 2 Garden Close, Stockwell Rd, London SW9 9TU

2 Quakers and peace

QPS, Friends House, Euston Road, London NW1 2BJ
PPU, Peace Education Project, 6 Endsleigh St, London WC1H ODX
Imperial War Museum, Lambeth Road, London SE1 6HZ
Centre for Peace Studies, St Martin's College, Lancaster
Concord Films Council, 201 Felixstowe Road, Ipswich, Suffolk IP3 9BJ
Pax Christi, St Francis of Assisi Centre, Pottery Lane, London W11 4NG

3 Saying 'No' to war

European Nuclear Disarmament (END), Bertrand Russell House, Gamble St, Nottingham NG7 4ET.
Fellowship of Reconciliation (FOR), 40-46, Harleyford Road, London SE11 5AY
World Disarmament Campaign, 238 Camden Road, London NW1 9HE
CND, 11 Goodwin Street, London N4 3HQ
Christian CND, 22-24 Underwood Street, London N1 7JG
Conservative Research Department, 32 Smith Square, Westminster, London SW1P 3HH
Nuclear Weapons Freeze, 82 Colston St, Bristol BS1 5BB

The Church and The Bomb (Working Party report; chair: Bishop of Salisbury) Hodder & Stoughton, 1982
Peace and War – A First Source Book by Chris Leeds, Stanley Thornes
The Nuclear Issue by W Wellington
Children of Hiroshima, Children of Hiroshima Publishing Committee 1981
Sadaka – The One Thousand Paper Cranes by Eleanor Coerr, Hodder & Stoughton, 1983
The Hiroshima Story by Maruki Toshi, A & C Black, 1983
New Internationalist Peace Pack from New Internationalist, Freepost, Oxford OX1 2BR

4 Peace Park

Faith in the City (A Call for Action by Church & Nation), Report of the Archbishop of
    Canterbury's Commission on Urban Priority Areas, Church House Publications, 1985
Child Poverty Action Group, 1 Macklin Street, London WC2 5NH
British Council of Churches Community Race Relations Unit, 2 Eaton Gate, London
    SW1W 9BL
Conservation Society, 12a Guildford St, Chertsey, Surrey, KT16 9BQ
Industrial Common Ownership Movement, 7-8 The Corn Exchange, Leeds LS1 7BP
Friends of the Earth, 377 City Road, London EC1V 1NA

6 Women

Bringing the Invisible Into the Light (Quaker Women's Group Swarthmore Lecture
    1987), Quaker Home Service, Friends House, Euston Road, London NW1 2BJ
Greater Expectations, Religious & Moral Education Press
World Studies 8-13: 'Making Global Connections: A World Studies Workbook',
    Longman Group
Women in Religion, Shap Mailing, 1989

8 Only human

United Nations Association, 3 Whitehall Court, London SW1
Minority Rights Group, 29 Craven Street, London WC2N 5NT
Amnesty International, 1 Easton Street, London WC1X 8DJ
International Society for Human Rights, 56 Sutherland Street, London SW1
Chile Committee for Human Rights, 266 Pentonville Road, London N1 9JY
Action by Christians against Torture, 32 Wentworth Hill, Wembley, Middlesex HA9 9SG

It's Not Fair by Anne Wilkinson, Christian Aid, PO BOX 1, London SW9 8BH (written
    for the International Year of Youth 1985)
Your Life – My Life – an introduction to Human Rights and Responsibilities by Sara
    Woodhouse, The Writers' and Scholars' Educational Trust